# A WORD TO
# FELLOW PASTORS
## and Other Christian Leaders

# Register This New Book

## Benefits of Registering*

- ✓  FREE **replacements** of lost or damaged books

- ✓  FREE **audiobook** – *Pilgrim's Progress,* audiobook edition

- ✓  FREE information about new titles and other **freebies**

www.anekopress.com/new-book-registration

*See our website for requirements and limitations.

# A WORD TO FELLOW PASTORS

## and Other Christian Leaders

### Things Every Minister of the Gospel Must Consider

## Horatius Bonar

We love hearing from our readers. Please contact us at www.anekopress.com/questions-comments with any questions, comments, or suggestions.

*A Word to Fellow Pastors and Other Christ-Followers* – Horatius Bonar
Revised Edition Copyright © 2019
First edition published 1875

Scripture quotations are taken from the Jubilee Bible, copyright © 2000, 2001, 2010, 2013 by Russell M. Stendal. Used by permission of Russell M. Stendal, Bogota, Colombia. All rights reserved.

*Cover Design: J. Martin*
*Cover Image: Lightspring/Shutterstock*
*Editors: Sheila Wilkinson and Ruth Clark*

Printed in the United States of America
Aneko Press

www.anekopress.com

Aneko Press, Life Sentence Publishing, and our logos are trademarks of
Life Sentence Publishing, Inc.
203 E. Birch Street
P.O. Box 652
Abbotsford, WI 54405

**RELIGION / Christian Ministry / Evangelism**

Paperback ISBN: 978-1-62245-619-2
eBook ISBN: 978-1-62245-620-8

10  9  8  7  6  5  4  3  2  1

Available where books are sold

# Contents

# Preface

It is not difficult to write a preface to this classic treasure of the Christian ministry, written by a Scottish Presbyterian theologian who was born in Edinburgh on December 19, 1808, and died there on July 31, 1889. He belongs to a previous generation, but his little manual is timeless, for it meets the needs of our day almost as accurately as it met the needs of the parish of Kelso in 1866 and later in Edinburgh.

Horatius Bonar was first of all a "winner of souls," although he was also a great preacher and a writer of some of our best hymns. He became moderator of the General Assembly of his church.

When we read his manual on how to win men for Christ, we are reminded, page after page, of his three best hymns, although he was the author of many. He could say, "I heard the voice of Jesus say," and therefore he could write the hymn beginning with those words.

How many have been led to Christ by this invitation to accept Him as their Savior? And how many Christians have rededicated themselves to their Lord and Master and recalled the day when they first loved Him, when they sang, "Here, O My Lord, I See Thee Face to Face" at Holy Communion?

Not only are his counsels to the winners of souls spiritual, divine, and searching, but the keynote of it all is that of urgency, as he expressed in his third great hymn, "Go, Labor On, Spend and Be Spent." The third stanza of that hymn ought to be written as a motto on the desk of every pastor:

> Go, labor on while it is day,
> > The world's dark night is hastening on.
> Speed, speed thy work, cast sloth away,
> > It is not thus that souls are won.

This is a book for winners of souls, not for loiterers on the highway or for slothful servants of our Master. It is a heart-searching book but also one that gives new courage to continue the daily task. Reprinted again and again by the American Tract Society, it is now issued by request in slightly abridged form.

There are two books that tell the story of Horatius

Bonar's life in detail. One is entitled *Horatius Bonar: a Memorial*, published in 1889, and the other is *Memories of Dr. Horatius Bonar, by Relatives and Public Men* (Edinburgh, 1909). Both have a portrait as a front-page illustration.

As a boy, I recall one little book that used to lie on my father's desk – that is sixty years ago – in his pastoral study in Michigan. It was his constant companion and was marked almost on every page. This little volume, bound in leather with gilt edges, had *Words to Winners of Souls* on the cover.

Samuel M. Zwemer, D.D., 1867-1952

New York City, March 3, 1950

'Tis not for us to trifle! Life is brief,
　　And sin is here.
Our age is but the falling of a leaf,
　　A dropping tear.
We have no time to sport away the hours,
All must be earnest in a world like ours.
Not many lives, but only one have we—

　　One; only one;—
How sacred should that one life ever be—
　　That narrow span!
Day after day, filled up with blessed toil;
Hour after hour, still bringing in new spoil.
　　– Dr. Horatius Bonar

## Chapter 1

# The Importance of Being Hot for Christ

H ow much more would a few good and fervent men effect in the ministry than a multitude of lukewarm ones!" said Oecolampadius, the German Reformer – a man who had been taught by experience and who has recorded that experience for the benefit of other churches and other days.

The mere multiplying of men calling themselves ministers of Christ will help little. They may only be "cumberers of the ground," hindrances to the work. They may be like Achan, troubling the camp; or perhaps like Jonah, raising the tempest. Even when sound in the faith, their unbelief, lukewarmness, and slothful formality may do irreparable injury to the cause of Christ, freezing and withering up all spiritual life around them. The lukewarm ministry of one who is theoretically orthodox is often more extensively and fatally ruinous to souls than that of one grossly inconsistent or flagrantly heretical. "What man on earth is so pernicious a drone [parasitic loafer] as an idle minister?" said Richard Cecil.[1] And John Fletcher remarked well that "lukewarm pastors made careless Christians."[2] Can the multiplication of such ministers be counted a blessing to a people?

When the church of Christ, in all her denominations, returns to its early example and walks in apostolic footsteps to seek to be conformed more closely to inspired models, she will turn to faithful leaders. When she allows nothing earthly to come between her and her living Head, then she will require the men to whom she entrusts the care of souls to be more distinguished by their spirituality, zeal, faith, and love than how learned and able they are.

In comparing Baxter and Orton, the biographer of the former remarked, "Baxter would have set the world on fire while Orton was lighting a match."[3] How true! Yet not only true of Baxter and Orton. These two individuals are representatives of two classes in the church of Christ in every age and every denomination. The latter class are by far the more numerous; the Ortons

---

1    Richard Cecil, *The Works of the Rev. Richard Cecil*, 1825.

2    John William Fletcher, *The Works of Reverend John Fletcher*, 1826.

3    William Orme, *The Practical Works of the Rev. Richard Baxter with a Life of the Author*, 1830.

you may count by hundreds, the Baxters by tens. Yet, who would not prefer a solitary specimen of the one rather than a thousand of the other?

## Baxter's Burning Sincerity

"When he spoke of weighty soul concerns," said his friend Matthew Sylvester at Baxter's funeral, "you might find his very spirit drenched therein."[4] No wonder he was blessed with such amazing success! Men felt that in listening to him they were in contact with one who was dealing with realities of an infinite moment.

This is one of the secrets of ministerial strength and ministerial success. And who can say how much of the overflowing infidelity of the present day is due not only to the lack of spiritual instructors – not merely to the existence of grossly unfaithful and inconsistent ones – but also to the coldness of many who are reputed to be sound and faithful? Men cannot help but feel that if religion is worth anything, it is worth everything; if it calls for any measure of zeal and warmth, it will justify the utmost degrees of these; and there is no consistent medium between reckless atheism and the most intense warmth of religious zeal. Men may dislike, detest, scoff at, and persecute the latter, but their

> Men cannot help but feel that if religion is worth anything, it is worth everything.

---

4    G. D. Boyle, *Richard Baxter*, 1883.

consciences are all the while silently reminding them that if there is a God and a Savior, a heaven and a hell, anything short of such life and love is hypocrisy, dishonesty, and perjury!

Thus, the lesson they learn from the lifeless discourses of the people we are alluding to is that since these men do not believe the doctrines they are preaching, there is no need of their hearers believing them. If ministers only believe them because they make their living by them, why should those who make nothing by them hesitate to deny them?

"Rash preaching," said Rowland Hill, "disgusts; timid preaching leaves poor souls fast asleep; bold preaching is the only preaching that is owned of God."[5]

It is not merely unsoundness in faith, nor negligence in duty, nor open inconsistency of life that mars the ministry and ruins souls. A man may be free from all scandal in either creed or conduct but may be a most grievous obstruction in the way of all spiritual good to his people. He may be a dry and empty cistern in spite of his orthodoxy. He may be freezing or blasting life at the very time he is speaking of the way of life. He may be repelling men from the cross even when he is proclaiming it in words. He may be standing between his flock and the blessing even when he is outwardly lifting up his hand to bless them. The same words that

---

5    Edwin Sidney, *The Life of the Rev. Rowland Hill, A.M.*, 1834.

would drop as the rain from warm lips, or refresh as the dew, fall from his lips as the snow or hail, chilling all spiritual warmth and blighting all spiritual life.

How many souls have been lost for lack of earnestness, solemnity, and love in the preacher, even when the words uttered were precious and true! *Feed the flock of God which is among you, caring for her, not by force, but willingly; not for shameful lucre, but with willing desire; and not as having lordship over heritage of the Lord, but in such a manner as to be examples of the flock* (1 Peter 5:2-3).

### A Most Important Objective: To Win Souls

We take for granted that the objective of the Christian ministry is to convert sinners and to edify the body of Christ. No faithful minister can possibly rest short of this. Applause, fame, popularity, honor, and wealth – all these are vain. If souls are not won, and if saints are not matured, our ministry itself is futile.

Applause, fame, popularity, honor, and wealth – all these are vain.

The question, therefore, which each of us has to answer to his own conscience is, Has it been the purpose of my ministry and the desire of my heart to save the lost and guide the saved? Is this my aim in every sermon I preach and in every visit I make? Is it under the influence of this feeling that I continually live and walk and speak? Do I pray and toil and fast and weep for this? Do I spend and am I spent for this, counting it, next to the salvation of my own soul, my greatest joy to be the instrument of saving others? Is it for this that I exist? To accomplish this, would I gladly die? Have I seen the pleasure of the Lord prospering in my hand? Have I seen souls converted under my ministry? Have God's people found refreshment from my lips and gone on their way rejoicing, or have I seen no fruit of my labors? Am I content to remain fruitless? Am I satisfied to preach without knowing of one saving impression I made or one sinner awakened?

Nothing short of positive success can satisfy a true minister of Christ. His plans may proceed smoothly, and his external machinery may work steadily, but without actual fruit in the saving of souls, he counts all these as nothing. His feeling is, *My little children, of whom I travail in birth again until Christ be formed in you* (Galatians 4:19). And it is this feeling that makes this true minister successful.

"Ministers," said Owen, "are seldom honored with success unless they are continually aiming at the conversion of sinners."[6] The resolution that in the strength and with the blessing of God the minister will never rest without success will insure it. It is the man who has made up his mind to confront every difficulty and

---

6    G. S. Bowes, *Illustrative Gatherings for Preachers and Teachers*, 1869.

counted the cost with his eye fixed on the prize that is determined to fight his way to that success. It is such a man that conquers, even as Paul did, for he said, *Thou has fully known my doctrine, conduct, purpose, faith, longsuffering, charity, patience, persecutions, afflictions, which came unto me . . . persecutions I have endured, and the Lord delivered me out of them all* (2 Timothy 3:10-11).

The dull apathy of other days is gone. Satan has actively taken the field, and it is best to meet him head-on. Besides, men's consciences are really on edge. God seems to be striving with them as before the flood. A breath of the divine Spirit has passed over the earth, and hence the momentous character of the time as well as the necessity for improving it as long as it lasts.[7]

The one true goal or resting place – where doubt and weariness, the stings of a pricking conscience, and the longings of an unsatisfied soul would all be quieted – is Christ Himself. Not the church, but Christ. Not doctrine, but Christ. Not forms, but Christ. Not ceremonies, but Christ. The resting place is Christ the God-man who gave His life for ours, sealed the everlasting covenant, and made peace for us through the blood of His cross. Christ is the divine storehouse of all light and truth, *In whom are hid all the treasures of wisdom and knowledge* (Colossians 2:3). Christ is the infinite vessel, filled with the Holy Spirit, the Enlightener, the

---

7    Bonar's comments on spiritual conditions in his day (1859) are strikingly appropriate for the present.

Teacher, the Quickener, and the Comforter, so that *of his fulness have all we received, and grace for grace* (John 1:16). This and this alone is the vexed soul's refuge, its rock to build on, and its home to abide in until the great tempter is bound and every conflict ended in victory, for *the LORD is my refuge, and my God is the rock of my trust* (Psalm 94:22).

## Meet Opinion with the Truth

Let us then meet this earnestness of the tempter, which is now the boast but may before long be the bane of the age, with that which alone can bring down its feverish pulse and soothe it into blessed calm – the gospel of the grace of God. All other things are just opiates, drugs, and quackeries. This is the divine medicine; this is the sole, speedy, and eternal cure. It is not by opinion that we are to confront opinion. The truth of God is what we are to wield; we are to apply the edge of the sword of the Spirit to the theories of man (which he proudly calls his opinions) and make him feel what a web of deception and folly he has been weaving for his own entanglement and ruin. *Stand firm, therefore, having your loins girt about with truth and having on the breastplate of righteousness, and your feet shod with the preparation of the gospel of peace, above all, taking the shield of faith, with which ye shall be able to quench all the fiery darts of the wicked* (Ephesians 6:14-16).

Opinions are not what man needs; he needs truth. Not theology, but God. Not religion, but Christ. Not literature and science, but the knowledge of the free love of God in the gift of His only begotten Son. Richard Baxter says:

I know not what others think, but for my own part, I am ashamed of my stupidity and wonder at myself that I do not deal with my own and others' souls as one that looks for the great day of the Lord. I wonder that I can have room for almost any other thoughts and words and that such astonishing matters do not wholly absorb my mind. I marvel how I can preach of them slightly and coldly and how I can let men alone in their sins. Why don't I go to them and beseech them for the Lord's sake to repent – however they may take it and whatever pain and trouble it should cost me?

I seldom come out of the pulpit but my conscience smites me that I have not been more serious and fervent. It accuses me not so much for lack of ornaments and elegancy, nor for letting slip an unhandsome word, but it asks me, "How could you speak of life and death with such a heart? How could you preach of heaven and hell in such a careless, sleepy manner? Do you believe what you say? Are you in earnest or in jest? How can you tell people that sin is such a thing, and that so much misery is upon them and before them and not be more affected with it? Shouldn't you weep over such a people, and shouldn't your tears interrupt your words? Shouldn't you cry aloud and show them their transgressions and entreat and beseech them as for life and death?"

Truly, this is the peal that conscience rings in my ears, and yet my drowsy soul will not be awakened. Oh, what a thing an insensible, hardened heart is! O Lord, save us from the plague of infidelity and hard-heartedness ourselves, or how shall we be fit instruments for saving others from it? *For the wages of sin is death, but the grace of God is eternal life in Christ Jesus our Lord* (Romans 6:23). Oh, do whatever need be on our souls that you would use us to do likewise for the souls of others![8]

---

8    *On the Ministry: Writings and Messages from the Puritans*, compiled and edited by Jon Bonker, 2014.

## Chapter 2

# The Importance of Being Right with God Ourselves

The true minister must be a true Christian. He must be called by God before he can call others to God. The apostle Paul states the matter as such: *God, who reconciled us to himself by Jesus Christ, and gave us the ministry of reconciliation* (2 Corinthians 5:18). They were first reconciled, and then they received the ministry of reconciliation. Are we ministers reconciled? It is only reasonable that a man who is to act as a spiritual guide to others should himself know the way of salvation. It has been frequently said that the way to heaven is blocked up with dead professors, but isn't it also true that the melancholy obstruction is not composed of members of churches only? Let us ministers take heed unto ourselves!

As the minister's life is in more than one respect the life of a ministry, let us speak a few words on ministerial holy living.

Let us seek the Lord early. *My voice shalt thou hear in the morning, O LORD; early will I present myself unto thee and wait* (Psalm 5:3). "If my heart is seasoned with His presence early, it will savor of Him all day long," said Bishop Joseph Hall to Lord Denny.[9] Let us see God before man every day. Robert McCheyne remarked:

> I ought to pray before seeing anyone. Often when I sleep late or meet with others early and then have family prayer and breakfast and forenoon callers, it is eleven or twelve o'clock before I begin secret prayer. This is a wretched system. It is unscriptural. Christ rose before day and went into a solitary place . . . Family prayer loses much power and sweetness, and I can do no good to those who come to seek for me. The conscience feels guilty, the soul unfed, the lamp not trimmed. Then, when secret prayer comes, the soul is often out of tune. I feel it far better to begin with God, to see His face first, and to get my soul near Him before it is near another. . . . It is best to have at least one hour alone with God before engaging in anything else. At the same time, I must be careful not to measure

---

9    *Anecdotes for the Family and the Social Circle*, compilation published by Gould, Kendall, and Lincoln, 1847.

communion with God by minutes or hours or by solitude.[10]

This true servant of Christ also exhorts a beloved brother: "Take heed to yourself. Your own soul is your first and greatest care. You know a sound body alone can work with power, much more a healthy soul. Keep a clear conscience through the blood of the Lamb. Maintain close communion with God. Study likeness to Him in all things. Read the Bible for your own growth first, then for your people."[11]

"With him," says his biographer, "the commencement of all labor invariably consisted in the preparation of his own soul. Before each day's visitations was a calm season of private devotion during morning hours. The walls of his chamber were witnesses of his prayerfulness – of his tears as well as of his cries. The pleasant sound of psalms often issued from his room at an early hour – then followed the reading of the Word for his own sanctification; few have so fully realized the blessing of the first psalm."[12] If only it were so with us all! "Devotion," said Bishop Hall, "is the life of religion, the very soul of piety, the highest employment of grace." It is much to be feared that "we are weak in the pulpit because we are weak in the closet."

10  Andrew A. Bonar, *Memoir and Remains of the Rev. Robert Murray McCheyne*, 1844.

11  Robert Steel, *Burning and Shining Lights, Or, Memoirs of Eminent Ministers of Christ*, 1864.

12  Andrew A. Bonar, *The Biography of Robert Murray M'Cheyne*, 1844.

## Walking with God

"To restore a commonplace truth to its first uncommon luster," writes Mr. Coleridge, "you need only translate it into action." Walking with God is a very commonplace truth. *Be ye therefore imitators of God, as dear children and walk in charity even as the Christ also has loved us and has given himself for us as an offering and a sacrifice to God for a sweet smelling savour* (Ephesians 5:1-2). Translate this truth into action – how splendid it becomes! The phrase, how time worn! The thing, how rare! It is such a walk – not an abstract ideal but a personality, a life, which the reader is invited to contemplate. Oh, that we would only set ourselves in earnest to partake in this rare work of transformation!

It is said of the energetic, pious, and successful John Berridge that "communion with God was what he enforced in the latter stages of his ministry. It was, indeed, his own meat and drink, and the banquet from which he never appeared to rise."[13] This shows us the source of his great strength. If we were always sitting at this banquet, it might be recorded of us before long, as it is of him, that "he was in the first year visited by about a thousand persons under serious impressions."[14]

---

13   Mary Grey Lundie Duncan, *History of Revivals of Religion in the British Isles*, 1836.

14   *The Scottish Christian Herald*, Vol. 1, 2nd series, 1839.

## Study the Speakers, Not the Sermons

To the men even more than to their doctrine we should point the eye of the inquirer who asks, Where did their success come from? Why can't the same success be ours? We may take the sermons of Whitefield or Berridge or Edwards for our study or our pattern, but the individuals themselves are what we must set before us. It is with the spirit of the men more than their works that we are to be instilled, if we are striving for a ministry as powerful and victorious as theirs. They were spiritual men who walked with God. *For those that are of the Christ have crucified the flesh with its affections and lusts. If we live by the Spirit, let us also walk in the Spirit* (Galatians 5:24-25). Living in fellowship with a living Savior is what transforms us into His image and fits us for being able and successful ministers of the gospel.

Living in fellowship with a living Savior is what transforms us into His image and fits us for being able and successful ministers of the gospel.

Without this, nothing else will profit. Not orthodoxy, or learning, or eloquence, or power of argument, or zeal, or fervor will accomplish anything without this. This is what gives power to our words and persuasiveness to our arguments, making them as either the balm of Gilead to the wounded spirit or sharp arrows of the mighty to the conscience of the stouthearted rebel.

From those who walk with Him in holy, happy communication, a virtue seems to go forth, and a blessed fragrance seems to surround them wherever they go. Nearness to Him, intimacy with Him, assimilation to His character – these are the elements of a ministry of power.

When we can tell our people, "We beheld His glory, and therefore we speak of it; it is not from report we speak, but we have seen the King in His beauty" – how lofty the position we occupy! Our power in drawing men to Christ springs chiefly from the fullness of our personal joy in Him and the nearness of our personal communion with Him. The countenance that reflects most of Christ and shines most with His love and grace is most fitted to attract the gaze of a careless, giddy world, and win restless souls from the fascinations of creature-love and creature-beauty. A ministry of power must be the fruit of a holy, peaceful, loving intimacy with the Lord.

## Faithfulness Essential to Success

*The law of truth was in his mouth, and iniquity was not found in his lips: he walked with me in peace and righteousness, and turned many away from iniquity* (Malachi 2:6). Let us observe the connection declared here to exist between faithfulness and success in the work of the ministry, between a godly life and the *turn*[ing] *many away from iniquity.* The reason we first became ministers as we declared at our ordination was the saving of souls; the reason we still live and labor is the same; the means to this end are a holy life and a faithful fulfillment of our ministry.

The connection between these two things is close and sure. We are entitled to depend upon it. We are called upon to pray and labor with the confident expectation of its being realized. And where it is not realized, we must examine ourselves with all diligence, in case the cause of the failure is in us, in our lack of faith, love, prayer, zeal, warmth, spirituality, or holiness of life – for by these the Holy Spirit is grieved. Success is attainable; success is desirable; success is promised by God. Nothing on earth can be more bitter to the soul of a faithful minister than the lack of success. To walk with God and be faithful to those entrusted to us is the sure way of attaining it. Oh, how much depends on the holiness of our lives, the consistency of our character, and the heavenliness of our walk and conversation!

> To walk with God and be faithful to those entrusted to us is the sure way of attaining it.

Our position is such that we cannot remain neutral. Our life cannot be one of harmless obscurity. We must either repel or attract – save or ruin – souls! How loud the call and how strong the motive to spirituality of soul and conscientiousness of life! How solemn the warning against worldly-mindedness and vanity, against flippancy and frivolity, against negligence, sloth, and cold formality!

Of all men, a minister of Christ is especially called to walk with God. Everything depends on this – his own peace and joy and his own future reward at the coming of the Lord. But God especially points to this as the true and sure way of securing the blessing. This is the grand secret of ministerial success. One who walks with God reflects the light of His countenance upon a darkened world, and the closer he walks, the more of this light he reflects. *For the God, who commanded the light to shine out of darkness, has shined in our hearts to bring forth the light of the knowledge of the clarity* [glory] *of God in the face of Jesus Christ* (2 Corinthians 4:6). One who walks with God carries in his very air and countenance a sweet serenity and holy joy that diffuses tranquility around. One who walks with God receives and imparts life wherever he goes; as it is written, out of him *shall flow rivers of living water* (John 7:38). He is not merely the world's light but also the world's fountain, dispensing the water of life on every side and making the barren waste to blossom as the rose. He waters the world's wilderness as he moves along his peaceful course. His life is blessed; his example is blessed; his communication is blessed;

his words are blessed; his ministry is blessed! Souls are saved, sinners are converted, and many are turned from their iniquity.

## Chapter 3

# The Danger of Unfruitful Ministry

*O my God, I am confused and ashamed to lift up my face to thee, my God: . . . O our God, what shall we say after this?* – Ezra 9:6, 10

The ministerial life of multitudes who are called to be overseers of the flock of Christ might be summed up as delivering sermons on each Lord's Day, administering the Lord's Supper, visiting those who occasionally request it, and attending religious meetings. An incumbency of thirty, forty, or fifty years often yields no more than this. So many sermons, so many baptisms, so many sacraments, so many visits, and so many meetings of various kinds are all the pastoral annals, the parish records, and the whole lifetime ministry to many! Such a record would make no mention of souls that have been saved.

Multitudes have perished under such a ministry; only the judgment will disclose whether any have been saved. There might be learning, but there was no *tongue of the wise, . . . to speak a word in season to him that is weary* (Isaiah 50:4). There might be wisdom, but it certainly was not the wisdom that wins souls. There might even be the sound of the gospel, but it seemed to contain no glad tidings at all. It did not come from warm lips to startled ears as the message of eternal life – *the glorious gospel of the blessed God* (1 Timothy 1:11). Men lived, but their minister never asked them whether they were born again! Men became sick, sent for the minister, and received a prayer on their deathbeds as their passport into heaven. Men died and were buried where all their fathers had been laid; there was a prayer at their funeral and decent respects paid to their remains, but their souls went to the judgment seat without thought or care. No man, not even the minister who had vowed to watch over them, had said to them, "Are you ready?" – or warned them to flee from the wrath to come.

Isn't this description too true of many districts and many ministers? We do not speak in anger; we do not speak in scorn; we ask the question solemnly and earnestly. It needs an answer. If ever there was a time when there should be *great searchings of heart* and frank acknowledgment of unfaithfulness, it is now when God is visiting us – visiting us in both judgment and mercy. We speak in brotherly kindness; surely the answer should not be of wrath and bitterness. And if this description is true, consider the sin that there must be in ministers and people! How great must be the spiritual desolation that prevails! Surely there is something grievously wrong in such a case – something that calls for solemn self-examination in every minister and requires deep repentance.

## The Tragedy of a Barren Ministry

Fields plowed and sown, but yielding no fruit! Machinery constantly in motion, but all without one particle of produce! Nets cast into the sea and spread wide, but no fishes caught! All this for years – for a lifetime! How strange! Yet it is true. There is neither fancy nor exaggeration in this matter. Question some ministers, and listen to other accounts they give. They can tell you of sermons preached, but of sermons blessed, they can say nothing. They can speak of discourses that were admired and praised, but of discourses that have been made effectual by the Holy Spirit they cannot speak. They can tell you how many have been baptized

> Machinery constantly in motion, but all without one particle of produce!

and how many communicants have been admitted, but of souls awakened, converted, and ripening in grace, they can give no account. They can enumerate the sacraments they have dispensed, but whether any of them have been *times of refreshing* or times of awakening, they cannot say. They can tell you what and how many cases of discipline have passed through their hands, but whether any of these have resulted in godly sorrow for sin or professed penitents being absolved by them to give evidence of being washed and sanctified and justified, they can give no information. They never thought of such a matter!

They can tell what the attendance at Sunday school is and what the abilities of the teacher are, but they do not know how many of these precious little ones whom they have vowed to feed are seeking the Lord. They don't know if their teacher is a man of prayer and piety. They can tell you the population of their parish, the number in their congregation, or the material well-being of their flocks, but they have no idea as to their spiritual state, how many have been awakened from the sleep of death, or how many are followers of God as dear children. Perhaps they would deem it rashness and presumption, if not fanaticism, to inquire. And yet they have sworn before men and angels to *watch for* [their] *souls* because they must give an account! But oh, of what use are sermons, sacraments, and schools if souls are left to perish, living religion is lost sight of, the Holy Spirit is not sought, or men are left to grow up and die – not pitied, not prayed for, and not warned?

### For God's Glory and Man's Good

It was not so in other days. Our fathers really watched and preached for souls. They asked and they expected a blessing – and they were not denied. They were blessed in turning many to righteousness. Their lives record their successful labors. How refreshing the lives of those who lived only for the glory of God and the good of souls. There is something in their history that compels us to feel that they were ministers of Christ – true watchmen.

*How refreshing the lives of those who lived only for the glory of God and the good of souls.*

How encouraging to read of Baxter and his labors at Kidderminster! How solemn to hear of Henry Venn and his preaching, for it is said that men "fell before him like slaked lime!"[15] And in the blest labors of that man of God – the apostolic George Whitefield – isn't there much to humble us as well as to stimulate us? We also read that Henry Tanner, who was himself awakened under Whitefield, "seldom preached one sermon in vain."[16] We are told that in their missionary tours throughout England, Berridge and Hicks were blessed

---

15    *The Christian Observer*, Vol. 59, 1859.
16    Robert Philip, *The Life and Times of the Reverend George Whitefield*, 1837.

in one year to awaken four thousand souls. Oh, for these days again! Oh, for one day of Whitefield again!

Thus, someone has written, "The language we have been accustomed to adopt is this: we must use the means but leave the event to God; we can do no more than employ the means. This is our duty, and having done this, we must leave the rest to Him who is the dispenser of all things." Such language sounds well, for it seems to be an acknowledgment of our own nothingness and a call to savor the submission to God's sovereignty. But it is only noise; it has no real substance in it, for though there is truth stamped on the face of it, falsehood lies at the root of it. To talk of submission to God's sovereignty is one thing, but to submit to it is another quite-different thing.

> To talk of submission to God's sovereignty is one thing, but to submit to it is another quite-different thing.

### Submission Involves Renunciation

Really to submit to God's sovereign disposal always involves the deep renunciation of our own will in the matter concerned, and such a renunciation of the will can never be effected without a soul being brought through severe and trying experiences of an inward and most humbling nature. Therefore, while we are quietly satisfied to use the means without obtaining the end, and this costs us no such inward pain and deep humbling as that alluded to, and if we think that we are leaving the affair to God's disposal, we deceive ourselves, and the truth in this matter is not in us.

No, to really give anything to God implies that the will, which is emphatically the heart, has been set on that thing. If the heart has indeed been set on the salvation of sinners as the end of the means we use, we cannot possibly give up that end without the heart experiencing severe and deep pain by the renunciation of the will involved in it. When, therefore, we can be quietly content to use the means for saving souls without seeing them saved, it is because there is no renunciation of the will – that is, no real submitting to God in the affair. The fact is, the will – that is, the heart – had never really been set upon this end. If it had, it could not possibly give up such an end without being broken by the sacrifice.[17]

### Covering Falsehood with Truth

When we can be satisfied to use the means without obtaining the end and speak of it as though

---

17    Henry James Prince, *The Charlinch Revival*, 1842.

we are submitting to the Lord's will, we use a truth to hide a falsehood, exactly in the same way that those formalists in religion do. They continue in forms and duties without going beyond them, though they know they will not save them. And when they are warned of their danger and earnestly entreated to seek the Lord with all the heart, they reply by telling us they know they must repent and believe, but they cannot do either one by themselves; they tell us they must wait until God gives them grace to do so.

Now, this is a truth, absolutely considered, but most of us can see that they are using it as a falsehood to cover and excuse a great insincerity of heart. We can readily perceive that if their hearts were really set upon salvation, they could not rest satisfied without it. Their contentedness is the result not of heart submission to God but of heart indifference to the salvation of their own souls.

It is exactly so with us as ministers when we can rest satisfied with using the means for saving souls without seeing them really saved or we ourselves being brokenhearted by it. At the same time, as we quietly talk of leaving the result to God's will, we make use of a truth to cover and excuse a falsehood, for our ability to leave the matter is not, as we imagine, the result of heart submission to God but of heart indifference to the salvation of the souls we deal with. No, truly, if the heart is really set on such an end, it must gain that end or break in losing it.[18]

He that saved our souls has taught us to weep over the unsaved. Lord, let that mind be in us that was in You! Give us Your tears to weep, for our hearts are hard toward our fellow men. We can see thousands perish around us, and our sleep might never be disturbed; no vision of their awful doom always scaring us, and no cry from their lost souls turning our peace into bitterness.

Our families, our schools, our congregations, our cities, our land, and our world might well send us to our knees every day, for the loss of even one soul is terrible beyond conception. Eye has not seen, nor ear heard, nor has entered the heart of man, what a soul in hell must suffer forever. *In that place shall be weeping and gnashing of teeth* (Luke 13:28). Lord, give us hearts of tender mercies! What a mystery! The soul and eternity of one man depends upon the voice of another!

---

18    Ibid.

Chapter 4

# The Importance of
# Eliminating Our Faults

*Remember therefore from where thou art
fallen, and repent, and do the first works;
or else I will come unto thee quickly, and
will remove thy lampstand out of his place,
except thou repent.* – Revelation 2:5

In the year 1651, the Church of Scotland drew up a humble acknowledgement of the sins of the ministry because, in regard to her ministers, they sensed "how deep our hand is in the transgression, and that the ministers have no small accession to the drawing on of these judgments that were upon the land." This document is a striking and searching one.[19] It

---

19  George Gillespie, *The Presbyterian's Armoury in Three Volumes*,
    Vol. 3, "A Humble Acknowledgement of the Sins of the Ministry of
    Scotland," 1846.

is perhaps one of the fullest, most faithful, and most impartial confessions of ministerial sin ever made. A few excerpts from it will introduce this chapter on ministerial confession.[20]

### Confessing Sins before Entrance to the Ministry

(1) Lightness and profanity in conversation, unsuitable to that holy calling which they did intend, not thoroughly repented of. (2) Corrupt education of some . . . not repented of. (3) Not studying to be *in Christ* before they are in the ministry, nor to have the practical knowledge and experience of the mystery of the gospel in themselves before they preach it to others. (4) Neglecting to fit themselves for the work of the ministry by not improving prayer and fellowship with God, education at schools, opportunities of a lively ministry, and other means, and not mourning for these neglects. (5) Not studying self-denial nor resolving to take up the cross of Christ. (6) Negligence to entertain a sight and sense of sin and misery; not wrestling against corruption nor studying mortification and restraint of spirit.

### Two Points on the Entrance to the Ministry

(1) Entering the ministry without respect to a commission from Jesus Christ, so that it has come to pass that many have run without being sent. (2) Entering

---

20  Editor's note: The following list is only a partial list of the sins that were confessed by the Presbyterian ministers. The numbers have therefore been changed, and each section starts over with number 1.

the ministry, not from the love of Christ nor from a desire to honor God in gaining souls, but for a name and for a livelihood in the world in spite of a solemn declaration to the contrary at admission.

## Sins after Entrance to the Ministry

(1) Ignorance of God, lack of nearness with Him, and taking up little of God in reading, meditating, and speaking of Him. (2) Exceedingly great selfishness in all that we do; acting from ourselves, for ourselves, and to ourselves. (3) Not caring how unfaithful and negligent others were, so it might contribute to our testimony of faithfulness and diligence, while being rather content, if not rejoicing, at their faults. (4) Experiencing little delight in those things that increase our nearest communion with God; sporadic in our walk with God and neglect of acknowledging Him in all our ways. (5) In going about duties, least careful of those things which are most remote from the eyes of men. (6) Seldom in secret prayer with God, except to fit us for public performance; and even that is much neglected or gone about very superficially.

## Excuses and Negligence

(1) Glad to find excuses for the neglect of duties. (2) Neglecting the reading of Scriptures in secret for our own edification as Christians; only reading them as

may fit us for our duty as ministers and often neglecting that. (3) Not given to reflecting upon our own ways, nor allowing conviction to have a thorough work upon us; deceiving ourselves by resting upon absence from and abhorrence of evils through the light of a natural conscience and looking upon this as an evidence of a real change. (4) Influence of evil on the heart and carelessness in self-searching, which make us unfamiliar with ourselves and estranged from God.

### Failure to Deny Self

(1) Not guarding nor wrestling against seen and known evils, especially our sense of power. (2) Drawn away with the temptations of the time and other particular temptations, according to our inclinations and fellowship. (3) Instability and wavering in the ways of God because of the fear of persecutions, hazards, or loss of esteem and declining duties because of the fear of jealousies and reproaches. (4) Not esteeming the cross of Christ and sufferings for His honorable name but rather shifting sufferings from self-love. (5) Deadness of spirit, after all the sore strokes of God upon the land.

(6) Little conscience for secret humiliation and fasting, by ourselves and in our families, so we might mourn for our own and the land's guiltiness and great backslidings; little public humiliation of our own hearts. (7) Finding our own pleasure when the Lord calls for

our humiliation. (8) Not taking to heart the sad and heavy sufferings of the people of God abroad and the lack of thriving of the kingdom of Jesus Christ and the power of godliness within.

## Hypocritical Thoughts and Actions

(1) Refined hypocrisy; desiring to appear what, indeed, we are not. (2) Studying more to learn the language of God's people than to exercise its precepts. (3) Artificial confessing of sin without repentance; professing to declare iniquity but not resolving to be sorry for sin. (4) Neglecting secret confession, even of those things that we are convicted of. (5) No reformation after solemn acknowledgments and private vows; thinking ourselves exonerated after confession. (6) More ready to search out and censure faults in others than to see or deal with them in ourselves.

## Self-Focus and Pride

(1) Accounting of our worth according to the estimation that others have of us. (2) Our estimation of men according to how they agree with or disagree with us. (3) Not fearing to meet with trials, but presuming to go through them unshaken in our own strength. (4) Not learning to fear from the falls of gracious men; nor mourning and praying for them. (5) Not observing particular punishments or improving on them for

the honor of God and the edification of ourselves and others. (6) Little or no mourning for the corruption of our nature, and less groaning under and longing to be delivered from that body of death, the bitter root of all our other evils.

## Our Conversation with Others

(1) Fruitless conversing with others – for the worse rather than for the better. (2) Foolish jesting away of time with impertinent and useless conversation very unbecoming to the ministers of the gospel. (3) Spiritual purposes often dying in our hands when they are begun by others. (4) Carnal familiarity with natural, wicked, and destructive men, whereby they are hardened, the people of God stumbled, and we ourselves blunted.

## Loving Pleasure More than God

(1) Neglecting fellowship with those by whom we might profit. (2) Desiring more to converse with those that might better us by their talents than with those that might edify us by their graces. (3) Not studying opportunities for doing good to others. (4) Shifting of prayer and other duties when asked – choosing rather to omit them than do them ourselves. (5) Abusing time in frequent recreation and pastimes and loving our pleasures more than God. (6) Taking little or no time for Christian conversation with young men trained

for the ministry. (7) Common and ordinary talk on the Lord's Day.

### Failure in Relationships

(1) Slighting Christian admonition from any in our flock or others as being below us, and ashamed to take any warning from private Christians. (2) Dislike of or bitterness against those who deal freely with us with admonition or reproof and not dealing faithfully with others who would welcome it from us.

(3) Not praying for men of a contrary judgment but using reservation and keeping a distance from them; being more ready to speak about them than to them or to God for them. (4) Not weighed with the failings and miscarriages of others, but rather taking advantage of them to justify ourselves. (5) Talking about and jesting at the faults of others rather than having compassion for them. (6) No painstaking work in the religious ordering of our families or being examples to other families in our congregation. (7) Hasty anger and passion in our families and conversation with others. (8) Covetousness, worldly-mindedness, and an inordinate desire for the things of this life, which cause a neglect of the duties of our calling and a distraction with the things of the world. (9) Lack of hospitality and charity to the members of Christ. (10) Not cherishing godliness in the people and even being afraid of it; hating

the people of God for their piety and attempting to quench the work of the Spirit among them.

## Trusting in Our Own Ability

(1) Not entertaining that edge of spirit in ministerial duties which we found at the beginning of our ministry. (2) Great neglect of reading and other preparation; or preparation merely literal and bookish, making an idol of a book, which hinders communion with God; or presuming on past assistance and praying little. (3) Trusting our gifts, talents, and pains taken for preparation, whereby God is provoked to blast good matter, though well-ordered and worded. (4) Careless in employing Christ and drawing virtue out of Him to enable us to preach in the Spirit and in power. (5) In praying for assistance, we pray more for assistance for the messenger than for the message that we carry, not caring what becomes of the Word if we have some measure of assistance in the duty. (6) The matter we bring forth is not seriously taken to God in prayer to be quickened (made alive or meaningful) for His people. (7) Neglect of prayer after the Word is preached.

## Fainthearted Preaching

(1) Failure to warn in our preaching of snares and sins in public affairs by some; and too much, too frequent, and unnecessary speaking by others about public business

and transactions. (2) Exceedingly great neglect and unskillfulness to explain the excellences and usefulness of and the necessity of an interest in Jesus Christ and the new covenant, which ought to be the great subject of a minister's study and preaching. (3) Speaking of Christ more by what others say than from knowledge and experience or any real impression of Him upon the heart. (4) Preaching that is too legalistic. (5) Lack of seriousness in preaching the gospel; not savoring anything except what is new, so that the essentials of religion are neglected.

(6) Not preaching Christ in the simplicity of the gospel, nor ourselves as the people's servants for Christ's sake. (7) Preaching of Christ, not so the people may know Him but that they may think we know much about Him. (8) Preaching about Christ's leaving of the world without a brokenness of heart or stirring ourselves to take hold of Him. (9) Not preaching with compassion to them who are in danger of perishing. (10) Preaching against public sins, neither in such a way nor for such an end as we ought – for the gaining of souls and drawing men out of their sins; but rather because it is to our advantage to say something of these evils.

## Attitude toward Others

(1) Bitterness, instead of zeal, in speaking against evil-doers, sectarians, and other scandalous persons and

the unfaithfulness in them. (2) Not studying to know the particular condition of the souls of the people so we may speak to them accordingly; nor keeping a particular record of them, though convinced of the usefulness of this. (3) Not carefully choosing what may be most profitable and edifying; lack of wisdom to discover which doctrine to apply to the conditions of souls to reinforce His Word and message. (4) Choosing texts on which we have something to say, rather than those needed by the conditions of souls and times; frequent preaching of the same things, so we may not be put to the work of new study. (5) Reading, preaching, and praying in such a way that we are distanced from God.

## Personal Shortcomings

(1) Too soon satisfied in the discharge of duties and holding off challenges of conscience with excuses. (2) Indulging the body and wasting much time in idleness. (3) Too much seeking our own credit and applause and being pleased when we get it and dissatisfied when it is lacking. (4) Timidity in delivering God's message; letting people die in reigning sins without warning. (5) Studying the discharge of duties more to free ourselves from censure than to approve ourselves to God.

(6) Not making all the counsel of God known to His people; particularly, not giving testimony in times of defection. (7) Not studying to profit by our own

doctrine or the doctrine of others. (8) For the most part, preaching as if we ourselves were not included in the message that we carry to the people. (9) Not rejoicing at the conversion of sinners, but content with the lifelessness of the Lord's work among His people; fearing, if they should thrive better, we would be more challenged and less esteemed by them.

(10) Many, in preaching and practice, diminish the power of godliness. (11) We preach, not as before God, but as to men; as evident by the different pains in our preparation to speak to our ordinary hearers and to others to whom we would approve ourselves. (12) Negligent, lazy, and sporadic visiting of the sick. If they are poor, we go once and only when sent for; if they are rich and of greater reputation, we go more often, even before being sent for. (13) Not knowing how to speak a word in season to the weary.

(14) Lazy and negligent in instructing. (15) Not preparing our hearts nor wrestling with God for a blessing for the message, because of the ordinariness and expected easiness of it whereby the Lord's name is misused and the people profit little. (16) Looking on that exercise as a work that is below us, and not determining to study a right and profitable way of instructing the Lord's people. (17) Selective in instruction, passing by those who are rich and of better quality, though many stand in great need of instruction. (18) Not waiting

upon and following the ignorant but often passionately upbraiding them.

These are solemn confessions – the confessions of men who knew the nature of the ministry they had entered, and who were desirous of approving themselves to Him who had called them that they might give their account with joy and not with grief.

## Confessing Our Shortcomings

Let us deal honestly with ourselves as these ministers did. Our confessions ought to be no less abundant and searching.

*We have been unfaithful.* The fear of man and the love of his applause have often made us afraid. We have been unfaithful to our own souls, to our flocks, and to our brethren – unfaithful in the pulpit, in visiting, in discipline, and in the church. In the discharge of every duty of our stewardship, there has been grievous unfaithfulness. Instead of the specific acknowledgement of the sin being reproved, there has been the vague allusion to it. Instead of the bold reproof, there has been the timid hint. Instead of the uncompromising condemnation, there has been the feeble disapproval. Instead of the unswerving consistency of a holy life whose uniform tenor would be a protest against the world and a rebuke of sin, there has been unfaithfulness in our walk and conversation and in our daily deportment and communication with others. Any degree of faithfulness that we have manifested on the Lord's Day is almost neutralized by the lack of discretion that our weekday life exhibits.

## Archbishop Ussher's Example

Few men ever lived a life so busy and so devoted to God as James Ussher, Archbishop of Armagh. His learning, habits of business, station, and friends all contributed to keeping his plate full; his was a soul that seemed continually to hear a voice saying, "Redeem the time, for the days are evil" (Ephesians 5:16). He began early, for at ten years of age he was converted by a sermon preached on Romans 12:1 – *Therefore, I beseech you brethren, by the mercies of God, that ye present your bodies in living sacrifice.* He was a painstaking, laborious preacher of the Word for fifty-five years.

Yet take note of him on his deathbed! He clung to Christ's righteousness alone and saw only sin and deficiency in himself, even after such a life. The last words he was heard to utter were around one o'clock in the afternoon, and these words were uttered in a loud voice: "But Lord, forgive me especially for my sins of omission." His biographer said he begged for forgiveness of sins of omission with his most fervent last breath – this man who was never known to lose an hour but employed the last shred of his life for his great Lord and Master![21] The very day he was stricken with his last sickness, he rose from writing one of his great works and went to visit a sick woman to whom he spoke so fitly and fully that you would have thought he spoke of heaven as he was headed there. Yet this man was oppressed with a sense of his omissions.

Reader, what do you think of yourself – your undone duties, your unimproved time, your lack of prayer, your shrinking from unpleasant work and putting it on others, and your being content to sit under your vine and fig tree without using all efforts for the souls of others? Remember Ussher's words: "Lord, forgive me especially for my sins of omission!"

Read the confession of Jonathan Edwards in regard to both personal and ministerial sins:

> Often I have had very persuasive views of my own sinfulness and vileness; very frequently to such a degree as to hold me in a kind of loud weeping, sometimes for a considerable time together, so that I have often been forced to shut myself up. I have had a vastly greater sense of my own wickedness and the badness of my heart than ever I had before my conversion. . . . My wickedness, as I am in myself, has long appeared to me perfectly ineffable, swallowing up all thought and imagination. . . . I know not how to express better

---

21    Charles Richard Elrington, *The Life of the Most Rev. James Ussher, D.D., Lord Archbishop of Armagh, and Primate of All Ireland*, 1848.

what my sins appear to me to be than by heaping infinite upon infinite and multiplying infinite by infinite. . . . When I look into my heart and take a view of my wickedness, it looks like an abyss infinitely deeper than hell. . . . And yet it seems to me that my conviction of sin is exceedingly small and faint: it is enough to amaze me that I have no more sense of my sin. . . . I have greatly longed of late for a broken heart and to lie low before God.[22]

## Worldliness Stunts the Conscience

We have been carnal and unspiritual. The tone of our life has been low and earthly. Associating too much and too intimately with the world, to a great measure we have become accustomed to its ways. Hence, our tastes have been perverted, our consciences blunted, and that sensitive tenderness of feeling that endures suffering and shrinks from sin has worn off and become a callousness that we once believed ourselves incapable of.

Perhaps we can call to mind a time when our views and aims were fixed upon a standard of almost heavenly elevation, and contrasting these with our present state, we are startled at the painful changes. And besides intimacy with the world, other causes have operated in producing this deterioration in the

---

22  Augustus Hopkins Strong, *Systematic Theology: A Compendium and Commonplace Book*, 1907.

spirituality of our minds. The study of truth as dogma more than in devotion has robbed it of its freshness and power. Daily, hourly occupation in the routine of ministerial labor has created formality and coldness. Continual working in the solemn duties of our office, such as dealing with souls in private about their eternal welfare or guiding the meditations and devotions of God's assembled people, often with little prayer and little faith, has tended grievously to rob us of that profound reverence and godly fear that ought to possess and pervade us. How truly and with what emphasis, we may say, *I am carnal, sold under sin* (Romans 7:14). The world has not been crucified to us, nor we unto the world; the flesh, with its members, has not been mortified. What a sad effect all this has had not only upon our peace of soul and our growth in grace but also upon the success of our ministry!

*We have been selfish.* We have shrunk from toil, difficulty, and endurance, counting not only our lives dear unto us but also even our earthly ease and comfort. We have sought to please ourselves instead of obeying Romans 15:2: *Let each one of us please his neighbour in that which is good, unto edification.* We do not bear *one another's burdens, and so fulfil the law of the Christ* (Galatians 6:2). We have been worldly and covetous. We have not presented ourselves unto God as *living sacrifices*, laying ourselves, our lives, our substance, our time, our strength, and our faculties – our all – upon His altar. We seem to have lost sight of this self-sacrificing principle on which Christians, but much more as ministers, we are called upon to act. We have had little idea of anything like sacrifice at all. Up to the point where a sacrifice was demanded, we may have been willing to go, but there we stood, counting it unnecessary, perhaps calling it reckless and unadvised, to proceed further. Yet, shouldn't the life of every Christian, especially of every minister, be a life of self-sacrifice and self-denial, even as the life of Him who *pleased not himself* (Romans 15:3)?

> We have had little idea of anything like sacrifice at all.

*We have been slothful.* We have been sparing of our effort. We have not endured hardness as good soldiers of Jesus Christ. Even when we have been instant *in* season, we have not been so *out* of season; neither have we sought to gather the fragments of our time so not a moment will be thrown idly or unprofitably away. Precious hours and days have been wasted in loafing, in visiting, in pleasure, and in idle or aimless reading that might have been devoted to the prayer closet, the study, the pulpit, or the meeting. Laziness, self-indulgence, and fickleness have eaten like a canker into our ministry, halting the blessing and marring our success.

It cannot be said of us, *For my name's sake* [thou]

*hast laboured, and hast not fainted* (Revelation 2:3). Alas! We have fainted – or at least grown *weary in well doing*. We have not been conscience about our work. We have not dealt honestly with the church to which we pledged the vows of ordination. We have dealt deceitfully with God, whose servants we profess to be. We have shown little of the unwearied, self-denying love with which, as shepherds, we ought to watch over the flocks committed to our care. We have fed ourselves but not the flock.[23]

*We have been cold.* Even when diligent, how little warmth and glow we have. The whole soul is not poured into the duty; hence, it too often wears the repulsive air of methodical routine. We do not speak and act like men in earnest. Our words are feeble, even when sound and true; our looks are careless, even when our words are weighty. Our tones betray the apathy which both words and looks disguise. Love is lacking – deep love, love strong as death, love such as made Jeremiah weep in secret places for the pride of Israel. Love like Paul's as he spoke *even weeping* for the enemies of the cross

---

23  Hear Richard Baxter's statement of his usual ministerial duties in answer to some enemies who taunted him with idleness: "The worst I wish you is that you had my ease instead of your labor. I have reason to take myself for the least of all saints, and yet I fear not to tell the accuser that in comparison to mine, I take the labor of most of the town's tradesmen to be a pleasure to the body, though I would not exchange it with the greatest prince. Their labor preserves health; mine consumes it. They work in ease; I in continual pain. They have hours and days of recreation; I have scarce time to eat and drink. Nobody molests them for their labor; the more I do, the more hatred and trouble I draw upon me." This is "spending and being spent"; this is an example worthy of imitation.

of Christ. In preaching and visiting, in counseling and reproving, what formality, what coldness, how little tenderness and affection we have! "Oh, that I was all heart," said Rowland Hill, "and soul, and spirit to tell the glorious gospel of Christ to perishing multitudes!"

### Afraid to Tell the Whole Truth

We have been timid. Fear has often led us to soften or generalize truths that would have brought hatred and reproach upon us if stated plainly. So, we have often failed to declare to our people the whole counsel of God. We have shrunk from reproving, rebuking, and exhorting with all long-suffering and doctrine. We have feared we might alienate friends or awaken the wrath of enemies. Hence, our preaching of the law has been feeble and restricted; our preaching of a free gospel has been more vague, uncertain, and tentative. Instead of being *bold in our God to announce unto you the gospel of God with much diligence* (1 Thessalonians 2:2), we are deficient in that majestic boldness and nobility of spirit which marked Luther, Calvin, Knox, and the mighty men of the Reformation. Of Luther it was said, "Every word was a thunderbolt."

> Fear has often led us to soften or generalize truths that would have brought hatred and reproach upon us if stated plainly.

We have been lacking in seriousness. In reading the lives of Howe or Baxter, Brainerd or Edwards, we are in company with men who in strictness of conduct and gravity of demeanor were truly of the apostolic school. We feel that these men must have carried weight with them, both in their words and their lives. We see also the contrast between ourselves and them in respect to that deep solemnity of air and tone which made men feel that they walked with God. How deeply we should be ashamed at our levity, frivolity, flippancy, vain mirth, foolish talking, and jesting by which grievous injury has been done to souls, the progress of the saints stifled, and the world affirmed in its wretched vanities.

## Preaching Self Instead of Christ

*We have preached ourselves, not Christ.* We have sought applause, courted honor, been greedy for fame and jealous of our reputation. We have preached too often to exalt ourselves instead of magnifying Christ and to draw men's eyes to ourselves instead of fixing them on Him and His cross. No, and haven't we often preached Christ for the very purpose of getting honor to ourselves? Christ, in the sufferings of His first coming and the glory of His second, has not been the Alpha and the Omega, the first and the last, of all our sermons.

*We have used words of man's wisdom.* We have forgotten Paul's resolution to avoid the enticing words of man's wisdom when he said, *For Christ sent me not to baptize, but to preach the gospel, not with wisdom of words, lest the cross of Christ should be made void* (1 Corinthians 1:17). And later he said, *We speak, not in the words which man's wisdom teaches, but with doctrine of the Holy Spirit, jointly fitting spiritual things by spiritual means* (1 Corinthians 2:13). We have reversed his reasoning as well as his resolution and acted as if we could brighten and beautify the cross by well-studied, well-polished, well-reasoned discourses and make it no longer repulsive. We have tried to make it irresistibly attractive to the carnal eye. Hence, we have often sent men home satisfied with themselves and convinced that they were religious because they were affected by our eloquence, touched by our appeals, or persuaded by our arguments. In this way, we have made the cross of Christ of no effect and sent souls to hell with a lie in their right hand. Thus, by avoiding the offense of the cross and the foolishness of preaching, we have had to labor in vain and mourn over an unblest, unfruitful ministry.

*We have not fully preached a free gospel.* We have been afraid of making it *too free*, lest men should be led into immorality – as if it were possible to preach too free a gospel or that its *freeness* could lead men into sin. Only a free gospel can bring peace, and only a free gospel can make men holy. Luther's preaching was summed up in

51

these two points: "We are justified by faith alone, and we must be assured that we are justified." This is what he urged his German Reformation brother Brentius to preach. *Justified therefore by faith, we have peace with God through our Lord Jesus, the Christ* (Romans 5:1). It was by such free, full, bold preaching of the glorious gospel, unhindered by works, merits, terms, and conditions, and unclouded by the fancied humility of doubts, fears, and uncertainties that such blessed success accompanied his labors. Let us go and do likewise. Connected to this is the necessity of insisting on the sinner's immediate turning to God and demanding in the Master's name the sinner's immediate surrender of his heart to Christ. Strange that sudden conversions should be so disliked by some ministers. They are the most scriptural of all conversions.

## Too Little Emphasis on God's Word

*We have not sufficiently studied and honored the Word of God.* We have given a greater prominence to man's writings, man's opinions, and man's systems in our studies than to the Word. We have drunk more out of human cisterns than divine, but *all scripture is given by inspiration of God and is profitable for doctrine, for reproof, for correction, for instruction in righteousness, that the man of God may be perfect, thoroughly furnished unto all good works* (2 Timothy 3:16-17). We have held more fellowship with man than God, even though He tells us to *be still, and know that I am God* (Psalm 46:10). Hence, the mold and fashion of our spirits, our lives, and our words have been derived more from man than God. We must study the Bible more; we must *study to show thyself approved unto God, a workman that has nothing to be ashamed of, rightly dividing the word of truth* (2 Timothy 2:15). We must steep our souls in it. We must not only lay it up within us but also transfuse it through the whole texture of the soul.

> We must study the Bible more.

*We have not been men of prayer.* The spirit of prayer has slumbered among us. The closet is seldom visited and delighted in. We have allowed business, study, or active labor to interfere with our prayer time. And the feverish atmosphere in which both the church and nation are enveloped has found its way into our prayer closet, disturbing the sweet calm of its blessed solitude. Sleep, company, idle visiting, foolish talking and jesting, idle reading, and unprofitable occupations exhaust time that might have been redeemed for prayer.

## Time for Everything but Prayer

Why aren't we concerned about getting time to pray? Why is there so little forethought in planning our time and work so as to secure a large portion of each day for prayer? Why is there so much speaking, but so little prayer? Why is there so much running to and fro, but so little prayer? Why so much bustle and business, but so little prayer? Why so many meetings with our fellow men, but so few meetings with God? Why so little being alone and so little thirsting of the soul for the calm, sweet hours of unbroken solitude, when God and His child hold fellowship together as if they could never part?

It is the lack of these solitary hours that not only injures our own growth in grace but also makes us unprofitable members in the church of Christ and renders our lives useless. In order to grow in grace, we must be much alone with God. It is not in society – even Christian society – that the soul grows most rapidly and vigorously. In one single quiet hour of prayer, the soul will often make more progress than in days of company with others. It is in the desert that the dew falls freshest and the air is purest. So with the soul.

*In one single quiet hour of prayer, the soul will often make more progress than in days of company with others.*

When none but God is near, His presence alone, like the desert air that is not mingled with the noxious breath of man, surrounds and pervades the soul, and the eye perceives the clearest, simplest view of eternal certainties. That is when the soul gathers in wondrous refreshment and power and energy.

In this way also we become truly useful to others. When we come out fresh from communion with God, we can go forth to do His work successfully. In the closet we get our vessels filled with blessing, so that when we come forth, we cannot contain it to ourselves but must pour it out wherever we go as a blessed necessity. We cannot say, as did Isaiah, *My lord, I stand continually all the day and all night long upon my watchtower* (Isaiah 21:8). Our life has not been like Samuel's while he was waiting for the voice of God: *Speak, LORD; for thy slave hears* (1 Samuel 3:9). This has not been the attitude of our souls and the guiding principle of our lives. Nearness to God, fellowship with God, waiting upon God, and resting in God have been too seldom the characteristics of our private or our ministerial walk. Therefore, our example has been powerless, our labors unsuccessful, our sermons weak, and our whole ministry fruitless and feeble.

## Seeking the Spirit's Strength

*We have not honored the Spirit of God.* It may be that we have recognized His role in words, but we have not kept this continually before our eyes and the eyes of the people. We have not given Him the glory that is due unto His name. We have not sought His teaching or His anointing – *the anointing of the Holy One, and ye know all things* (1 John 2:20). Neither in the study of the Word or the preaching of it to others have we rightfully acknowledged His office as the Enlightener of understanding, the Revealer of truth, and the Testifier and Glorifier of Christ. We have grieved Him by the dishonor done to Him as the third person of the glorious Trinity; and we have grieved Him by slighting His office as the Teacher, the Convincer, the Comforter, and the Sanctifier. Therefore, He left us to reap the fruit of our own perversity and unbelief. Furthermore, we have grieved Him by our inconsistent walk, lack of discretion, worldly-mindedness, unholiness, prayerlessness, unfaithfulness, lack of seriousness, and a life and conversation that are weak in conformity to the character of a disciple or the office of ambassador.

An old Scottish minister once wrote this about himself:

> I find a lack of the Spirit – of the power and demonstration of the Spirit – in praying, speaking, and exhorting by which men are mainly convinced and are an amazement and a wonder unto others. So they stand in awe of them and that glory and majesty by which respect and reverence are procured. This demonstration of the Spirit, which made Christ's sermons different from those of the scribes and Pharisees, I judge to be the beams of God's majesty and of the Spirit of holiness breaking out and shining

through His people. But my foul garments are on! Woe is me! The crown of glory and majesty is fallen off my head; my words are weak and carnal, not mighty, so contempt is bred. There is no remedy for this but humility, self-loathing, and a striving to maintain fellowship with God.

## Too Little Imitation of Christ

*We have had little of the mind of Christ.* We have come far short of the example of the apostles, and much shorter of that of Christ. We are far behind the servants and much farther behind the Master.

> *In humility let each esteem others better than themselves, with each one not looking to their own things, but also to the things of others. Let this mind be in you, which was also in Christ Jesus, who, being in the form of God, thought it not robbery to be equal with God, but emptied himself, taking the form of a slave, made in the likeness of men, and being found in fashion as a man, he humbled himself and became obedient unto death, even the death of the cross.*
> (Philippians 2:3-8)

We have had little of the grace, the compassion, the meekness, the lowliness, and the love of God's eternal

Son. His weeping over Jerusalem has caused us little heartfelt sympathy. His *seeking of the lost* is seldom imitated by us. His unwearied *teaching of the multitudes* we shrink from as too difficult for flesh and blood. His days of fasting and His nights of watchfulness and prayer are not fully realized as models for us to copy. His counting not His life dear unto Him that He might glorify the Father and finish the work given to Him is but little remembered by us as the principle on which we are to act. Yet surely, we are to follow His steps; the servant is to walk where his Master has led the way; the under-shepherd is to be what the Chief Shepherd was. We must not seek rest or ease in a world where He whom we love had none.

> We must not seek rest or ease in a world where He whom we love had none.

## Chapter 5

# The Need of Revival in Ministry

It is easier to speak or write about revival than to achieve it. There is so much rubbish to be swept out, so many self-imposed hindrances to be dealt with, so many old habits to be overcome, so much laziness and easy-mindedness to be contended with, so much ministerial routine to be broken through, and so much crucifixion of self and of the world to be undergone. As Christ said of the unclean spirit that the disciples could not cast out, so we may say, *This kind can come forth by nothing, but by prayer and fasting* (Mark 9:29).

After lamenting the evils of his life and his ministry, a minister in the seventeenth century resolved to set about their renewal:

(1) In imitation of Christ and His apostles and to get good done, I purpose to rise early every morning.

(2) As soon as I am up, to prepare some work to be done with a plan of how and when to do it; then to engage my heart to it, and in the evening to hold myself accountable and mourn over my failings.

(3) To spend a sufficient portion of time every day in prayer, reading, meditating, and spiritual exercises – in the morning, midday, evening, and before I go to bed.

(4) Once a month, at the end or in the middle of it, to keep a day of fasting and prayer for the public condition, for the Lord's people and their sad condition, and for raising up the work and people of God.

(5) To spend one day every six months for my own private condition in fighting against spiritual evils, making my heart more holy, or accomplishing some special exercise.

(6) Once every week to spend four hours over and above my daily portion in private for some special causes relating to either myself or others.

(7) To spend some time on Saturday evening for preparation for the Lord's Day.

(8) To spend six or seven days together, once a year, when most convenient, wholly and only on spiritual concerns.

## Today's Need for Revival

Such was the way in which this minister set about personal and ministerial revival. Let us take an example
from him. If he needed it much, we need it more.

In the fifth and sixth centuries, Gildas and Salvian
arose to alert a careless church and a formal ministry.[24] In
the sixteenth century, the same task faced the Reformers.
In the seventeenth century, Baxter and others took a
prominent part in stimulating the
lethargic devotion and dormant
energy of his fellow ministers. In
the eighteenth century, God raised
up some choice and noble men
to awaken the church and lead
the way to a higher and bolder

It is distressing to
see the amount of
ministerial fatigue and
inefficiency that still
spreads over our land.

career of ministerial duty. The present century stands
no less in need of some such stimulating influence.
We have experienced many symptoms of life, but still
the masses are not quickened. We require some new
Baxter to arouse us by his voice and his example. It is
distressing to see the amount of ministerial fatigue
and inefficiency that still spreads over our land. How
long, O Lord, how long?

The infusion of new life into the ministry ought
to be the objective of more direct and special effort as
well as of more united and fervent prayer. The prayers

24  Cortlandt Van Rensselaer, ed., *Home, the School, and the Church*,
1850.

of Christians ought to be more directed to the students, the preachers, and the ministers of the Christian church. It is a *living* ministry that our country needs, and without such a ministry, it cannot long expect to escape the judgments of God. We need men who will spend and be spent – who will labor and pray – who will watch and weep for souls.

### How Myconius Learned His Lesson

According to Melchior Adam, in the life of Myconius, the friend of Luther, we have the following beautiful and striking account of an event which proved to be the turning point in his history and led him to devote his energy to the cause of Christ:

The first night that he entered the monastery, intending to become a monk, he dreamed, and it seemed as if he was working a vast wilderness alone. Suddenly a guide appeared and led him onwards to a most lovely vale, watered by a pleasant stream of which he was not permitted to taste and then to a marble fountain of pure water. He tried to kneel and drink, when a crucified Savior stood before him, from whose wounds gushed the copious stream. In a moment, his guide flung

> We need men who will spend and be spent – who will labor and pray – who will watch and weep for souls.

him into the fountain. His mouth met the flow-ing wounds, and he drank most sweetly, never to thirst again!

No sooner was he refreshed than he was led away by his guide to be taught what great things he was yet to do for the Crucified One whose precious wounds had poured the living water into his soul. He came to a wide stretching plain covered with waving grain. His guide ordered him to reap. He excused himself by saying that he was unskilled in such labor. "What you know not, you shall learn," was the reply. They came nearer, and he saw a solitary reaper toiling at the sickle with such tremendous effort as if he were determined to reap the whole field himself. The guide ordered him to join this laborer, and seizing a sickle, showed him how to proceed.

Again, the guide led him to a hill. He surveyed the vast plain beneath him, and wondering, he asked how long it would take to reap such a field with so few laborers. "Before winter, the last sickle must be thrust in," replied his guide. "Proceed with all your might. The Lord of the harvest will send more reapers soon." Wearied with his labor, Myconius rested for a little. Again, the Crucified One was at his side, wasted and marred in form. The guide laid his hand on Myconius and said, "You must be conformed to Him."

With these words, the dreamer awoke. But he awoke to a life of zeal and love. He found the Savior for his own soul, and he went forth to preach of Him to others. He took his place by the side of that noble reaper, Martin Luther. He was stimulated by his example and toiled with him in the vast field until laborers arose on every side, and the harvest was reaped before the winter came.[25]

The lesson to us is to thrust in our sickles. The fields are white, and they are wide in compass; the laborers are few, but there are some devoted ones toiling there already. In other years, we have seen Whitefield and Hill putting forth their enormous efforts, as if they would reap the whole field alone. Let us join such men, and the Lord of the harvest will not leave us to toil alone.

### Reaping the Great Harvest

"When do you intend to stop?" was the question once put by a friend to Rowland Hill. "Not until we have carried all before us," was the prompt reply. Such is our answer too. The fields are vast, the grain whitens, and the harvest waves. Through grace, we shall go

25    Cortlandt Van Rensselaer, ed., *Home, the School, and the Church,* 1850.

forth with our sickles, never to rest until we lie down where the Lamb Himself shall lead us – by the living fountains of waters where God will wipe off the sweat of toil from our weary foreheads and dry up all the tears of earth from our weeping eyes. Some of us are young and fresh; we may still have many days in the providence of God. These must be days of strenuous, ceaseless, persevering, and, if God blesses us, successful toil. We will labor until we are worn out and laid to rest.

> We will labor until we are worn out and laid to rest.

Thomas Vincent, the non-conformist minister, in his small volume on the great plague and fire in London entitled *God's Terrible Voice in the City*, gave a description of the manner in which the faithful ministers who remained amidst the danger discharged their solemn duties to the dying inhabitants. He wrote of the manner in which the terror-stricken multitudes hung with breathless eagerness upon their lips to drink in salvation before the dreaded plague had swept them away to the tomb. Church doors were flung open, but the pulpits were silent, for there was none to occupy them. Most hirelings had fled.

## Preaching to Plague Victims

Then, God's faithful band of persecuted faithful came forth from their hiding places to fill the forsaken pulpits.

They stood up in the midst of the dying and the dead to proclaim eternal life to men who were expecting death before the next day. They preached in season and out of season. Weekday or Sunday was the same to them. The hour might be authorized or random; it didn't matter. They did not preach on nice points of ecclesiastical regularity or irregularity; they lifted up their voices like trumpets with unwavering confidence.

Every sermon could be their last. Graves were lying open around them; now life seemed not merely a hand-breadth but a hairbreadth away. Death was nearer than ever, and eternity emerged in all its vast reality. Souls were precious, and opportunities were no longer to be trifled away. Every hour possessed a value beyond the wealth of kingdoms; the world was a passing, vanishing shadow, and man's days on earth had been cut down from seventy years to the twinkling of an eye.

Oh, how they preached! No polished periods, no learned arguments, and no labored paragraphs chilled their appeals or rendered their speech unintelligible. No fear of man, no love of popular applause, no ever-scrupulous dread of strong expressions, and no fear of excitement or enthusiasm prevented them from pouring out the whole passion of their hearts that yearned with tenderness unutterable over dying souls. Vincent said:

> Old Time seemed to stand at the head of the
> pulpit with his great scythe, saying with a hoarse

voice, "Work while it is called today; at night
I will mow thee down." Grim Death seemed
to stand at the side of the pulpit with its sharp
arrow, saying, "You shoot God's arrows, and I
will shoot mine." The grave seemed to lie open
at the foot of the pulpit with dust in her bosom,
saying –

"Louden thy cry
   To God,
   To men,
And now fulfill thy trust;
Here thou must lie –
   Mouth stopped,
   Breath gone,
And silent in the dust."

Ministers now had awakening calls to seriousness and intensity in their ministerial work to
preach on the side and brink of the pit into which
thousands were tumbling. There was such a vast
crowd of people in the churches where these ministers preached that many times they could not
come near the pulpit doors because of the masses.
The people were forced to climb over the pews to
the ministers. Such faces were seen in the assem-
blies as seldom seen before in London; such eager

looks, such open ears, such greedy attention – as
if every word would be eaten which dropped
from the mouths of the ministers.

## Should We Ever Be Less Earnest?

Thus they preached and thus they heard in those days
of terror and death. Men were in earnest then, both
in speaking and hearing. There was no coldness, no
fatigue, no studied oratory. Truly, they preached as
dying men to dying men. But the question is, Should it
ever be otherwise? Should there ever be less passion in
preaching or less eagerness in hearing than there was
then? True, life was a little shorter then, but that was
all. Death and its issues are still the same. Eternity is
still the same. The soul is still the same. Only one small
element was thrown in then that does not always exist
to such an extent – namely, the increased shortness of
life. But that was all the difference.

## Unbelief Weakens Our Testimony

Why then should our preaching be less impassioned,
our appeals less affectionate, our persistence less urgent?
We are a few steps farther from the shore of eternity;
that is all. Time may be a little stronger than it was
then, but only a very little. Its everlasting issues are still
as momentous and unchangeable. Surely, our unbelief
makes the difference. Unbelief makes ministers cold

in their preaching, lazy in visiting, and negligent in all their sacred duties. Unbelief chills the life and restricts the heart. Unbelief makes ministers handle eternal realities with irreverence. Unbelief makes them ascend with a light step to "that awful place – the pulpit,"[26] to deal with immortal beings about heaven and hell.

Note one of Richard Baxter's appeals:

I have been ready to wonder, when I have heard such weighty things delivered, how people can restrain from crying out in the congregation and much more how they can rest until they have gone to their ministers and learned what they should do. Oh, that heaven and hell should work no more upon men. Oh, that everlastingness should work no more! Oh, how can you withhold when you are alone to think of what it is to be everlastingly in joy or in torment? I wonder that such thoughts do not interrupt your sleep, and that those thoughts don't come to your mind when you are working. I wonder how you can do almost anything else; how you can have any quietness in your minds; how you can eat, drink,

---

26  A late minister used to say that he always liked to go from his knees to that awful place — the pulpit. Truly an awful place, a place where any degree of warmth is excusable, and where coldness is not only unjustifiable, but also horrible. "I love those that thunder out the Word," said Whitefield. "The Christian world is in a deep sleep. Nothing but a loud voice can awaken them out of it."

or rest until you have some assurance of everlasting comfort.

Is there a man or a corpse that is not affected with matters of this importance? That is more ready to sleep than to tremble when he hears how he must stand at the judgment of God? Is there a man or a clod of clay that can rise or lie down without being deeply affected with his everlasting estate? That can follow his worldly business but make nothing of the great business of salvation or damnation – even when he knows it is hard at hand? Truly, sirs, when I think of the weight of the matter, I wonder at the very best of God's saints upon earth that they are no better and do no more in so serious a matter. I wonder at those whom the world considers more holy than necessary, and scorns for making too much ado that they can put off Christ and their souls with so little reason. I wonder that they don't pour out their souls in every supplication, that they are not more taken up with God, and that their thoughts are not more serious in preparation to give their accounts. I wonder that they are not a hundred times more strict in their lives and more laborious and unwearied in striving for the crown than they are.

## Ready to Tremble

And for myself, as I am ashamed of my dull and careless heart and of my slow and unprofitable course of life, the Lord knows I am ashamed of every sermon I preach. When I think about what I have been speaking of, who sent me, and that men's salvation or damnation is dependent on it, I am ready to tremble in case God should judge me as a slighter of His truths and the souls of men. I fear that I should be guilty of their blood even in the best sermons. I think we should not speak a word to men in matters of such consequence without tears or the greatest earnestness that we possibly can. If we were not too guilty of the sin that we reprove, it would be so.

We are not in earnest either in preaching or in hearing. If we were, could we be so cold, so prayerless, so inconsistent, so lazy, so worldly, and so unlike men whose business is all about eternity?

We must remember that *faith comes by hearing, and the ear to hear by the word of God* (Romans 10:17).

We must work.

We must be more in earnest if we want to win souls. We must be more in earnest if we want to walk in the footsteps of our beloved Lord, or if we want to fulfill the vows that are upon us. We must be more in earnest if we want to be less than hypocrites. We must be more in earnest if we want to finish our course with joy and obtain the crown at the Master's coming. We must work *while it is day: the night comes, when no one can work* (John 9:4).

# Horatius Bonar – A Brief Biography

Born on December 19, 1808, Horatius Bonar was one of eleven children of James Bonar and Marjory Pyott Maitland Bonar. For several generations his ancestors had been ministers of the gospel.

Bonar graduated from the University of Edinburgh where Dr. Thomas Chalmers laid the foundation for solid learning, which continued through the years. This gave Bonar direction and strength during his most impressionable years. He was ordained in 1838 and accepted North Parish, Kelso, as his first parish. In addition to Dr. Chalmers, he allied himself with William C. Burns and Robert Murray McCheyne as spiritual mentors and friends.

As a young pastor, Bonar preached in villages and farmhouses throughout his district, for he saw

evangelization in a different light from his other con-
temporaries. To him, Christ had to come first, not
numbers of converts. In his house-to-house visitation,
he proved himself as a comforter of the sorrowful and
a guide for the confused. Colossians 3:23 was the verse
he lived by: *Whatsoever ye do, do it heartily, as to the
Lord, and not unto men.*

In 1843, he joined the Free Church of Scotland
after the "Disruption." The old church with its civil
service pastors had failed to arouse the faith of the
nation. This disruption was a schism in the Church
of Scotland where about 450 evangelical ministers
broke away over an issue of the church's relationship
with the state. There was disagreement about whether
the church was sovereign within its own domain with
Christ as Head or if the king was head. In this way, it
was similar to the Lutheran Reformation.

Those who left forfeited their livelihood, pulpits, and
aid from the established church to found and finance
a new national church from scratch. They needed to
train clergy and form a new college, which opened in
1843, with Dr. Chalmers as the first principal. Most of
the protest principles were conceded by Parliament by
1929, which paved the way for reunification.

In 1843, Horatius Bonar married Jane Catharine
Lundie. Together they had nine children, but five of
them died before adulthood – three in infancy. One

surviving daughter was later widowed with five children, so she moved back with her parents. Horatius said, "God took five children from life some years ago, and He has given me another five to bring up for Him in my old age."

In 1851, he wrote *Man: His Religion and His World* because he was concerned that pastors were diluting the gospel to make it pleasant and easier to accept. He always contended for the truth and never neglected pastoral work and preaching.

Horatius Bonar received an honorary degree of Doctor of Divinity from the University of Aberdeen and then visited Palestine on a mission to the Jews in 1856, which gave him the inspiration for the hymn "The Voice from Galilee," better known as "I Heard the Voice of Jesus Say." Revival had sprung up in Scotland while he was away, and he came back with a renewed interest in prophecy and a firm belief in the personal coming and reign of Jesus Christ. He did not believe that the world was getting better and civilization could save the world. Teachings of the coming of Christ, the tribulation, and the thousand-year reign had been lost, and the nineteenth-century preachers had to bring these doctrines back.

Bonar spoke as a dying man to dying men, resulting in many conversions. He wrote the *Kelso Tracts* to warn the careless, to present salvation simply, and to edify the saints. The tracts had wide circulation in Scotland, England, and America. In 1867, Bonar moved to Edinburgh to take over Chalmers' Memorial Church, and in 1883, he was elected moderator of the General Assembly of the Free Church of Scotland. Bonar continued to express his views in *Prophetical Landmarks* (1847) and served as editor of *The Quarterly Journal of Prophecy* (1848-1873) and the *Christian Treasury* (1859-1879). He even wrote biographies of ministers like *The Life of the Rev. John Milne of Perth* and *The Life and Works of the Rev. G. T. Dodds.*

Other books and tracts that bear his name are *Night of Weeping, The Everlasting Righteousness,* and *How Shall I Go to God?* Until his death, he warned about trends he saw creeping in and threatening the Christian church. In one of his last books – *Our Ministry: How It Touches the Questions of the Age* – he observed that "Man is now thinking out a Bible for himself, framing a religion in harmony with the development of liberal thought, constructing a worship on the principles of taste and culture, and shaping a God to suit the expanding aspirations of the age."

Horatius Bonar is best known as the principle hymn writer of Scotland. He was called the "prince of Scottish hymn writers." As he worked with young people, he realized they lacked enthusiasm. Even though he lacked an ear for music, he knew familiar tunes and wrote new words to them for the children. His experiment worked and the children became interested in the verses that were written for them personally. Because they were full of sound teaching, many adults loved to sing them also and requested to use them in other churches. He always granted permission for any church to use his hymns as long as they did not change his words.

He wrote more than six hundred hymns, and many hymnbooks carry these songs. Several are completely compiled from his hymns. The three volumes of *Hymns of Faith and Hope* contain a multitude of his hymns. While "I Heard the Voice of Jesus Say" and "My Redeemer Liveth" were two of the best known, he is largely remembered for his hymns that were based strongly on theology and doctrine, such as "Done is the Work That Saves" and "No Blood, No Altar Now." He wrote of justification, sanctification, the second coming, and the exaltation of Christ.

His hymns are childlike yet manly, hopeful but sympathetic. For many years they were mostly used by churches of other denominations but not his own. The Free Church of Scotland was opposed to singing at worship anything but metrical psalms and paraphrases.

Bonar believed "life is a journey, not a home; a road, not a city of habitation." He stated that "It is not the opinions that man needs; it is truth. It is not theology; it is God. It is not religion; it is Christ. It is not literature and science; but the knowledge of the free love of God in the gift of His only begotten Son." From the first day of his ministry until his last sermon, he closed with these words: "In such an hour as ye think not, the Son of Man cometh."

# Similar Titles

**The Soul Winner, by Charles H. Spurgeon**

As an individual, you may ask, *How can I, an average person, do anything to reach the lost?* Or if a pastor, you may be discouraged and feel ineffective with your congregation, much less the world. Or perhaps you don't yet have a heart for the lost. Whatever your excuse, it's time to change. Overcome yourself and learn to make a difference in your church and the world around you. It's time to become an effective soul winner for Christ.

As Christians, our main business is to win souls. But, in Spurgeon's own words, "like shoeing-smiths, we need to know a great many things. Just as the smith must know about horses and how to make shoes for them, so we must know about souls and how to win them for Christ." Learn about souls, and how to win them, from one of the most acclaimed soul winners of all time.

*Available where books are sold and free as an eBook*

**The Greatest Fight, by Charles H. Spurgeon**

This book examines three things that are of utmost importance in this fight of faith. The first is *our armory*, which is the inspired Word of God. The second is *our army*, the church of the living God, which we must lead under our Lord's command. The third is *our strength*, by which we wear the armor and use the sword.

The message in this book, when originally presented by Charles Spurgeon in his final address to his own Pastor's College, was received rapturously and enthusiastically. It was almost immediately published and distributed around the world and in several languages. After Charles Spurgeon's death in 1892, 34,000 copies were printed and distributed to pastors and leaders in England through Mrs. Spurgeon's book fund. It is with great pleasure that we present this updated and very relevant book to the Lord's army of today.

*Available where books are sold and free as an eBook*

**_Words of Counsel,_ by Charles H. Spurgeon**

Is there any occupation as profitable or rewarding as that of winning souls for Christ? It is a desirable employment, and the threshold for entry into this profession is set at a level any Christian may achieve – you must only love the Lord God with all your heart, soul, and mind; and your fellow man as yourself. This work is for all genuine Christians, of all walks of life. This is for you, fellow Christian.

_Available where books are sold and free as an eBook_

***How to Bring Men to Christ,*** **by Reuben A. Torrey**

*How to Bring Men to Christ* sheds light on how to reach the lost with the gospel – not *new* light, but *tested* and *true* light. Reuben A. Torrey will show you how to use appropriate, applicable Bible passages to reach every kind of lost individual. Regardless of the angle the lost may use to try to justify why they remain in their sad condition, Torrey offers Scripture passages and biblical principles that have proven to reach even the most stubborn of the unsaved.

*Available where books are sold and free as an eBook*

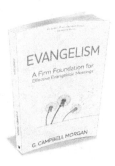

**_Evangelism,_ by G. Campbell Morgan**

Outside of personally living for and loving the Lord, there is arguably no greater work Christians can undertake than preaching the good news of Jesus Christ to the lost. It may be that you do not yet have that burden on your heart, or perhaps eternity itself is not yet a reality to you. Or, perhaps you have that burden, but feel like there are no open doors for ministry available to you. Your church may be cold and currently making no great impact in your community.

No matter your current circumstance, only believe that the same One who commissions His people for His work also has sufficient resources to enable the work to move forward. Only believe that as you dig into the Scriptures, perhaps with the help of this book, which serves as a biblical guide, that the One who cares most for this work can also put that same burden and love into the hearts of you and your church.

*Available where books are sold and free as an eBook*